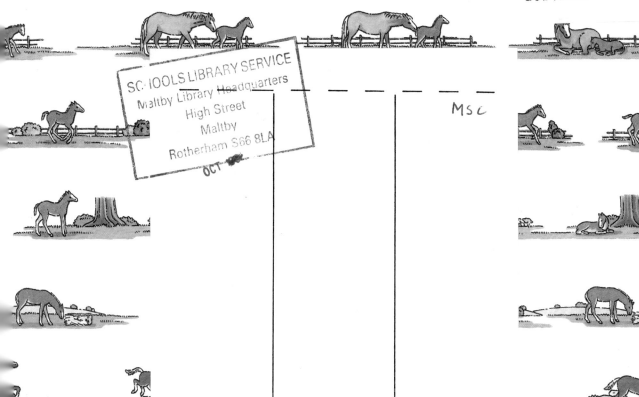

MSC

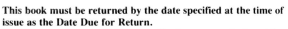

ROTHERHAM PUBLIC LIBRARIES

This book must be returned by the date specified at the time of
issue as the Date Due for Return.
The loan may be extended (personally, by post or telephone) for
a further period, if the book is not required by another reader,
by quoting the above number   LM1 (C)

A DORLING KINDERSLEY BOOK

Written and edited by Mary Ling
Art Editor Helen Senior
Production Louise Barratt
Illustrator Jane Cradock-Watson

Special thanks to Alison Mountain and Tito

First published in Great Britain in 1992 by
Dorling Kindersley Limited, 9 Henrietta Street, London WC2E 8PS

A CIP catalogue record for this book is available
from the British Library

ISBN 0-86318-868-0

Colour reproduction by J. Film Process Ltd, Singapore
Printed in Italy by L.E.G.O.

SEE HOW THEY GROW

FOAL

photographed by

GORDON CLAYTON

DORLING KINDERSLEY
London • New York • Stuttgart

Newborn

I am a foal. I have just been born. My legs are very wobbly.

My mother feeds me with her warm milk as soon as I struggle to my feet.

I feel much better
after my milk. My
legs are stronger.

In the meadow

I am one week old. I grow taller every day.

I spend my days in the meadow with my mother.

I cuddle close
to her when the
wind blows.

I love feeling
the soft grass
beneath my
hooves.

Looking for mum

I am two weeks old.
I have two new teeth.
I want to show
my mother.

Where is she? I
neigh loudly
to her.

10

I hope she
hears me.

My mother soon
comes. She is never
very far away.

Come and play

I am five weeks old.

I am very excited today.
A friend is coming to play.

We play our
games and run
around the field.

When we are
tired, we graze
together.
Playing with
friends is fun.

Crunchy apples

I am eight weeks old. I
gallop around the
fields each day.

Running about makes
me feel very hungry.

Here are some crunchy red apples. They smell good. I wonder if I can eat one?

15

Long legs

I am four months old. My coat is chestnut brown now.

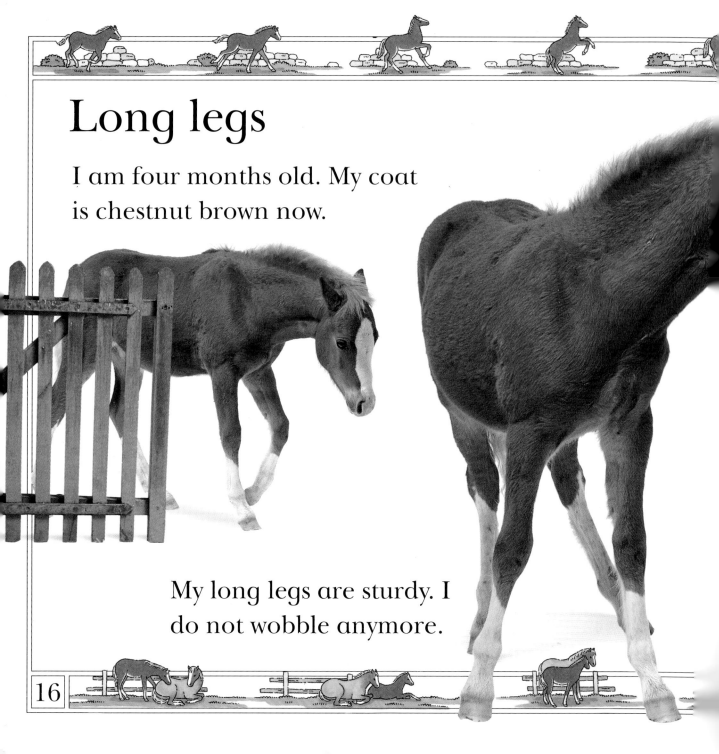

My long legs are sturdy. I do not wobble anymore.

I am growing taller every day.

I am almost as tall as my mother.

17

In the paddock

I am five months
old and nearly
fully grown.

18

Soon I will be big enough to join the other ponies in the paddock.

See how I grew

Newborn

One week old

Two weeks old   Five weeks old   Eight weeks old

Four months old   Five months old